THE
KIDS' BOOK
OF QUESTIONS

THE KIDS' BOOK OF QUESTIONS

<< NEW EDITION >>

Gregory Stock, Ph.D.

WORKMAN PUBLISHING · NEW YORK

Library of Congress Cataloging-in-Publication Data is available.

ISBN: 978-0-7611-8464-5

Cover illustration by Colleen AF Venable

Workman books are available at special discounts when purchased in bulk for premiums and sales promotions as well as for fund-raising or educational use. Special editions or book excerpts can also be created to specification. For details, contact the Special Sales Director at the address below or send an email to specialmarkets@workman.com.

Workman Publishing Co., Inc.
225 Varick Street
New York, NY 10014-4381
workman.com

WORKMAN is a registered trademark of Workman Publishing Co., Inc.

Printed in the United States of America

First printing February 2015

10 9 8 7 6 5 4

To Sadie,
the princess of my heart.

* * * * * * * * *

To Ben the king,
Aliza the queen, and Paul, Miranda,
Liffie, Kippie, Zach, Scott, Sam, Ben,
and Jake the minnow catcher.

INTRODUCTION

Most of the questions you are asked at school have right and wrong answers: Who invented the steam engine? What is the capital of Italy? How is blue cheese made? Such questions have answers you can always find in books or on the Internet, so it doesn't really matter if you sometimes don't know the answers.

The questions here do not have answers you can find in such places because they are about you. Knowing what you believe in and who you are is important, so look into yourself to find answers to these questions. This is not a test, though; no one answer is right for everyone. Here, there are no correct answers—only honest ones—and you are the only one who really knows how honest you are being. Don't say what you think others want you to; respond the way you actually feel.

The Kids' Book of Questions is for kids, but it is not a book of childish questions. Some questions are playful, even downright silly. Others are serious and focus upon the hard dilemmas you face in growing up. They raise issues about dealing with authority, understanding friendship, handling social pressures, overcoming fears, and deciding what's right and wrong. You will face these issues throughout your life.

Growing up is not easy these days. Kids are not sheltered from divorce, crime, drugs, sex, violence, and other things that are hard even for adults to deal with. You get a lot of advice from your family, friends, teachers, and even from television and movies; but different people tell you different things about what you should and shouldn't do.

What is right? Where do you fit into the world? Who can you trust? A big part of growing up is learning to make choices for yourself.

Thinking about questions like the ones in this book is a good way of practicing to do just that. When you use your imagination to explore difficult dilemmas, you can learn from situations without going through them in real life. So throw yourself into these questions and pretend they're real. When you care about a decision, the process of deciding will bring you new thoughts, ideas, and opinions that are entirely your own. Take this chance to discuss the things you feel most strongly about instead of everyday matters you've already talked about dozens of times.

With some of these questions you have to pretend you have extraordinary powers or are in strange and unusual situations. With others, you must remember your past or imagine your future. Treat these questions as your own. Play with them, add to them, change them, but don't cheat by trying to figure out ways to keep from having to make hard choices, because you will only be cheating yourself. And don't just answer yes or no—or let others get away with that. Try to figure out why you feel the way you do, and push others to do the same, because the reasons behind people's answers are often even more interesting than the answers themselves.

Playing with questions like these is a game to laugh and have fun with. It can also be a bit uncomfortable, because sometimes it is not easy to look at yourself and think about the kind of person you are, what you want, and what you care about. Talking about your thoughts and feelings with your friends will be a big help when you face difficult and confusing questions in this book, and when you next face tough choices in the real world. Just remember that growing occurs not from having answers but from searching for them.

A big difference between questions about things and questions about people is that you are never quite sure where personal questions will lead. Maybe that is why personal questions are so much fun. This book gives you an easy, playful way of raising issues you've wanted to talk about but haven't known how to bring up. Make full use of the chance and use these questions by yourself, with your friends, or even with adults.

Start asking the questions you find here, and similar questions of your own, and you'll soon be having lively discussions. I hope this new edition helps you see how sweet it can be to ask thought-provoking questions. It is amazing where one little question can take you. Good luck and have fun.

THE
KIDS' BOOK
OF QUESTIONS

If you ruled the
world and could have
anything you wanted,
and people would do
anything you wanted, do you
think you'd get **greedy**
and mean or be
good and fair?

Do you think
boys
or **girls** have it
easier?

3

If your mother promised to be home at 2:00 in the afternoon to take you to the movies but didn't show up until suppertime and didn't even phone, what would be a good punishment for her? Would punishing her be likely to make her be on time in the future?

4

If all your best friends were willing to be absolutely honest and tell you exactly what they most liked and disliked about you, would you want them to?

Would you
rather have
a **strict** teacher
who was **fair**
and taught you a lot
or one who was
relaxed and **fun**
but didn't
teach you much?

6

One day your father gets a really weird idea and dyes his hair green and puts a ring through his nose. Knowing everyone would be looking at him and snickering, would you go shopping with him if he wanted your company?

7

When you make a mistake, do you make up excuses? If so, do you think people believe you?

If you could have a
round-trip ride in a
time machine
and travel any distance
into the past or future,
where would you
want to go?

If a friend had an
important secret
and didn't want other people
to learn about it, would
telling you the secret be
a mistake?

10

If your parents were worried about a serious problem that had nothing to do with you directly, would you want them to tell you about it or would you rather not know?

11

What would you do if everyone in your family forgot your birthday?

When you find
yourself sitting in front of
awful-tasting food
that you're supposed to eat,
what's your best trick for
getting rid of it without
getting **caught?**

13

If you were alone
and had only a few minutes
to hide from **crooks** who
were about to break into your
house, where would
you hide? What is the
best **hiding place**
in your house?

14

Some adults have a lot of trouble enjoying themselves. If you were asked to give them some advice about how to play and have more fun, what would you say?

15

Is there any particular moment in your past you wish had been captured on video? Would you like to have more videos and photos from when you were younger?

16

Who do you dislike the most? What is the best thing about that person?

17

How would you act differently if you had a younger sister who idolized you and tried to copy everything you did? What things do you think your parents do only because they want to set an example for you? Do you think they have done things they won't tell you about because they're worried you might try to copy them?

18

If you could be
invisible
for a day,
what would
you **do?**

19

When did you
get yourself in the
biggest mess by telling
a lie? What do
you think would have
happened if you'd told
the truth?

20

If you could choose
any **bedtime**
you wanted for the
next year, **what time**
would you pick?

Are there things you
pretend not to like
but really do **enjoy**—for
example, being kissed by
your parents or having a
little sister tag along with
you? If so, why do you hide
your **feelings?**

22

When you're mad at your parents and want to get back at them, what's the best trick you have for getting on their nerves?

23

If you had to guess two things you'll like in a few years but don't like now, what would you guess? Pretend that if you are correct you will win $1,000.

24

If you could take either
a pill that made you
braver or one that
made you **stronger,**
which would you choose
and why? Would you rather
just stay as you are?

25

If you knew that by being the teacher's pet for two years you'd lose your friends and be teased by everyone, but later in life would be happy, successful, and admired by everyone, would you do it?

26

Do you think you have too many chores? If you were the one assigning chores in your house, what would you give yourself to do?

27

If your parents said they were going to have another baby and thought you were so terrific that they'd clone an identical twin of you, would you like or hate the idea? What do you think would be the worst thing about it? The best?

28

Would you rather your mom or dad give you more presents or spend more time with you? Which would make you feel more loved?

29

If you were offered $250
to kiss someone
you liked in front of
your whole class,
would you do it?

30

If you had a dog you really loved, and a mean neighbor killed it just because it pooped on his lawn, what do you think should happen to the person?

31

What is the
worst **nightmare** you
can remember? Would you
be willing to have the same
dream tonight if you
could spend a week at
Disneyland with
your friends?

32

If you woke up tomorrow and by magic were grown up and had kids of your own, how would you treat them differently than your parents treat you?

33

How would you feel if you found out today you were adopted as a baby? Would you try to find your biological parents?

34

If you agreed to sell
your bike to a **friend**
and someone later offered
you **more money,**
would you try to back
out of the deal?

If you and your friends
were collecting money for
a **charity,** and your
friends decided to **steal**
what they were collecting
and said they wouldn't be
friends with you
unless you joined them,
what would you do?

36

If you could be as
talented
as some friend of
yours at any one
thing, what would
you **choose?**

37

Would you rather wear the same uniform to school every day or wear anything you want? What would you wear if no one paid any attention to the way you dressed?

38

Clean your room! Take a bath! Wash your hands! Why do you think adults care so much about cleanliness?

39

If you told your
friends everything
about yourself, including the
things you are most
embarrassed by, do
you think they'd like you
less or more than
they do now?

40

Are you in a hurry to grow up? What does it mean to be "grown up," and when do you think it will happen to you?

41

While on vacation, you go to the beach with a friend's parents and people there are bathing nude. Would you want to stay and look or leave?

42

If everyone stopped **growing** and getting **stronger** when they reached your age, so adults were neither bigger nor stronger than you, would you **still** do what they said? If so, why?

43

If you had only five minutes to think up a **nickname** for yourself and knew everyone would use it for years, what would you **pick?** What name would you pick for your **best friend?** Your parents?

44

Imagine that your
principal told
you she wanted to make
school **better** and would
change it in any
one way you suggested.
What would you
tell her to do?

45

Of all the things you've heard about God and religion, what do you think is true and what do you think might be just a story?

46

If you could permanently trade lives with one of your classmates, brothers, or sisters, would you? If so, who would you pick and why?

47

If you could
change
any one thing about
your **parents,**
what would it be?

48

What things do you
think kids should be
punished for,
and how should it be done?
Is there an age when people
are too old to be punished
for the **mistakes** they
make? If so, what age
and why?

49

What are you
most proud
of having done?
What would make you
even **prouder?**

50

If everyone in your
class but you would be
killed unless you agreed to
sacrifice your own life,
would you **save** everyone
else or save yourself?
Would it matter if no one
would ever know about
what you had done?

51

What do you like most about your best friend? How long do you think it would take to make another best friend if you moved away?

52

Would you rather be very poor but have parents who loved you and each other, or be fabulously wealthy but have parents who ignored you and were always fighting with each other?

53

If someone
pulled down
a friend's **pants**
at a movie theater,
would you
laugh along
with everyone else?

54

What is the most boring thing you can imagine doing? Would you do it for a whole week if you could then celebrate your birthday twice each year?

55

What is the biggest difference between what happens on television and what happens in the real world?

56

Is there anyone
you **trust** so much
that you wouldn't be
afraid to have him or
her know every single
thought you have?

Would you be willing
to never again get
any gifts or surprises
if instead you could just
ask for anything you wanted
and have your parents
immediately
buy it for you?

58

What makes you feel guilty? Do people try to make you feel guilty very often?

59

If someone a lot smaller than you kept teasing you and telling lies about you and wouldn't stop, how far would you be willing to go to make the person stop? What about someone bigger than you?

Have you ever thought you were going to die—for example, in a big **thunderstorm** or a car accident? If so, did the **experience** teach you anything you could tell your **friends?**

61

When was the
last time you
were so **mad** at a friend
that you **screamed?**
Do you think you get over
your **anger** more quickly
when you show how
mad you are or when
you hide it?

62

Which subjects at school do you think will be completely useless when you get older? Which ones do you think will be important?

63

Would you spend two days all alone in your house if you knew nothing bad would happen and you could have any present you wanted afterward?

64

When was
the last time
you told your **parents**
you **loved** them?
When was the last time
they told you?

65

Are there certain kinds
of stealing—or
borrowing without
permission—that are
all right and others that
aren't? If so, what is the
difference between
them? When was the last
time you stole something or
thought about stealing
something?

66

What is the
hardest
thing about
**growing
up?**

67

When someone says
you are just like
your **mom** or **dad,**
do you like it? Do you try
more to be like your parents
or to be **different**
from them?

Would you rather
hang around with a group
of younger kids and be the
boss but do things younger
kids do, or hang around with
a group of older kids and be
the squirt but do things
older kids get to do?

69

What was the most exciting thing you ever did on a dare? Are you glad or sorry you did it?

70

Would you eat a worm sandwich if you'd get to be on your favorite TV show or meet your favorite movie star or musician?

71

Would you like
your parents to **cuddle**
and hug each other more
or less than they do now?
What about having them
hug and **kiss** you more
or less than now?

If you **found** a purse
or wallet on the playground
with a lot of **money**
in it, and no one saw you
pick it up, what
would you **do?**

If you could take
a **pill** that made you
sick for a week, but
kept you **healthy** for
an extra ten years when you
got old, would you want it?
What if it didn't make you
sick or if it made
you really sick for
a whole month?

74

Is there any argument you have again
and again with your dad or mom or
grandparents? If so, is there anything
you could do to prevent it? Do you
sometimes just enjoy arguing?

75

What's the luckiest thing that ever
happened to you?

76

If you liked someone who later turned out to be a liar, would you still want to be friends?

77

What advice would you give to a friend whose parents were getting a divorce and always trying to make him or her take sides in their arguments?

78

Did you ever
stand up
for something you thought
was **right** even though
a lot of people got upset with
you? If not, do you think
you could be **strong**
enough to do so?

When you're
at school,
do you **act** like a
different person
than when you're with
your **family?**

80

What things are too personal to discuss
with your parents? Is there anyone you
can talk to about these things?

81

Do you have many mementos, souvenirs,
and photographs? If so, how much
money would someone have to give you
to get you to throw them all away?

82

What is something you love doing now but will probably not enjoy in two years?

83

On Halloween, a group of high-school students are caught scaring little kids and stealing their candy. If you could decide the punishment, what would it be?

84

Would you rather be a
rich and **famous**
movie star or a great doctor
who **saves** a lot of people
but is not wealthy
or well-known?

85

Have you ever seen your parents drunk or very ill? How did it feel to see them that way?

86

Of all the nice things someone could truthfully say about you, which one would make you feel the best?

87

What is the
worst word you know?
How did you **learn** it
and when was the
last time you **said** it?

88

When was the last time you laughed at yourself because you did something silly or stupid?

89

If you could have one of your friends do anything you wanted and be your slave for a day, what would you ask for? Pretend he or she wouldn't get upset no matter what it was.

90

If you could make
your **parents** try
any one **food,** what
would it be?
Do you think **kids**
should be forced to
try new foods?

91

If this Saturday
you could do absolutely
anything in the
world you wanted,
what would you do?

92

Who is your biggest hero? Why do you
think this person is so terrific?

93

When was the last time you lied to your
parents? To a close friend? When was
the last time you got caught lying?

94

What tricks do your friends use to get you to do things they know you don't want to do?

95

Do you pick your nose or bite your nails? If so, do you think you always will, or will you stop one day?

What, if anything, have **adults** told you that you think might not be **true?** Do you think they actually **believed** what they were saying?

97

If you could change any one thing about the way you look, what would it be?

98

If your pet needed an expensive operation and could have it only if you agreed to give up Christmas and birthday presents for two years, would you do it?

Are you afraid to
ask questions when
you don't understand
something? For example,
do you somctimes
fake a laugh
when you don't
understand a joke?

100

What is the best
costume you ever wore?
Would you like getting
dressed up in
costumes every week if
you could?

101

Have you and your friends ever picked on people and made fun of them until they cried? If so, why did you do it? Did you enjoy it?

102

Are there things your parents won't do, but still make you do because it's supposed to be "good for you"? If so, do you think this is fair?

If an older kid hit
you, stole something
of yours, and then said
he'd hurt you if you
told on him, would you tell
anyone? If so, who?

104

Are you more likely to hold back your tears when you feel like crying or to hold back your laughter when you see something funny? Why?

105

Do you wish your parents would question you less or more about what you do and how you feel?

106

If your parents told you your best friend was no good and you couldn't see him or her anymore, how would you feel? Would you do what they said?

107

Have you ever farted and blamed someone else for it?

108

If you knew you wouldn't get **caught,** would you cheat on a test by **copying** someone's answers? What would you think if you saw other people **cheating?**

109

When was the last
time you did something
for a **stranger**
just to be **nice?**
What did you do?

If it would save
the lives of ten kids in
another country, would you
be willing to have really
bad acne for a year?
What about not getting
any new clothes
for a year?

111

If you knew your **best friend** had stolen something from a **neighbor,** and your father asked you what you knew about it, would you **lie** to protect your friend?

112

What is your
biggest fear? How would
your life be different
if suddenly you
weren't afraid of
this anymore?

113

If you knew that by practicing hard every Saturday you could become the best in your school at whatever you wanted, what—if anything—would you work on? Imagine it is twenty years from now and you are looking back on the choice you just made. Do you think you'd wish you had picked something else to work on?

114

If your parents lost their jobs and you had to try to help support your family, what would you do to earn money?

115

If you could pick any one **food** and have as much of it as you **wanted**—but nothing else—during the next week, what would you **pick**?

What would
make you try harder in
school: wanting to please
a **teacher** you liked,
not wanting to disappoint
your **parents,** or being
offered a fabulous
prize if you
did well?

117

How important is it for you to win?
When was the last time you cheated in
a game so you could win?

118

If you got so angry at your parents
that you decided to run away, where
would you go? If you ran away, do you
think you'd ever come home again?

119

If there was a hard but **exciting** project to do, would you rather do it by yourself and get all the **credit,** or work with your friends knowing that everyone would **share** the credit? What would it feel like to do it the other way?

120

What's the most
embarrassing
thing that ever happened
to you? Are you embarrassed
now by the same
things that used to
embarrass you?

121

Whose **room** would you most like to spend the afternoon looking through? Pretend you had **permission** to look at all the **private** possessions there.

122

Would it be worse to have to stay in your room for a week with a phone, computer, and TV, or to be able to go anywhere you want but have all electronic devices be off-limits?

123

Do your parents try to trick you into doing things? If so, do you usually figure out what's going on right away or not until later?

124

If you could grow up to be famous and successful, what would you like to be known for? Do you think you'll be famous someday?

125

If you had to either always rush and do things a lot more quickly than you do now, or always take your time and do things a lot more slowly than you do now, which would you prefer? Does it bother you more to be around people who are much faster or much slower than you are?

126

If you could do one
thing you're not **allowed**
to do yet because you're
supposedly **too young,**
what would it be?

127

When were you
last in a **fight?**
What would you be
willing to fight about
that doesn't directly
threaten you?

128

If you could choose to be the most attractive, the most athletic, or the smartest kid in your school, which would you want to be?

129

What do you think your parents worried about when they were your age? What do you think they worry about now?

130

If you could have any one magical power, what would you pick?

131

If a friend showed you how to access websites intended strictly for adults, would you go to them? What do you think you might find there that would be dangerous or difficult to handle? Do you like having adult sites blocked on your computer?

If you could
take a genetic test
to discover what things
you'd be best at, would
you want to take it or just
find out for yourself
over time?

133

If you could have either a wonderful new experience or a wonderful new possession, which would you want? Why?

134

Would you rather be average in height or the tallest in your class?

135

What kinds of
teasing do you
think you'd miss most
if everyone agreed to
never tease
you again?

136

What do you think your friends like most about you? If you lost that quality, do you think they'd still like you?

137

Adults can do more, but they have more responsibilities. Children can play more, but they get told what to do. Do you think kids or adults have a better deal?

138

If you could make
a TV show or website
about **anything** you
wanted and knew that
millions of people
would see it, what would
it be about?

Would you
rather have a job you
didn't like that paid a
lot or a job you loved
that paid just enough
to get by on?

140

If you could see into the future but not change anything, would you want to take a look?

141

What is the wildest and craziest thing you've ever done? Would you like to do it again?

142

Have you ever gotten yourself into a
mess by telling people you could do
things you really couldn't?

143

If your two best friends got so mad at
each other that they both refused to
come to your birthday party if the other
one was going to be there, what would
you do?

If you were mad at
your **brother** and
found out about something
bad he'd done, would you
tell your parents and get
him in **trouble?**

145

Would you like to have a watch with a HELP button you could press to immediately summon the police anytime you were in danger? Can you think of a time you could really have used something like that?

If one morning you
woke up and found that
during the night you'd
been **magically
transformed** into an
adult, what would you do?
Pretend you know you
will become a kid again
in one week.

147

If your principal decided to put tiny video cameras in all the classrooms so parents could go online anytime and watch their kids, would the idea bother you? How would having cameras like that everywhere change the way you feel about school?

148

If you could somehow make any one person in the world absolutely adore you, who would you pick? Does anyone like you now who you wish didn't?

If you couldn't watch TV for a year, what do you think you'd do with all the **extra time?** Do you think you'd be better off if you got to watch **more** TV than you do now, or if you had to watch **less** of it? Why?

150

Are you worried about what kind of place the **world** will be when you grow up? If so, what worries you most and what do you think could be done to **improve** things?

151

If you knew that by cheating you could win an important competition for your school and be a hero, would you? Pretend you were sure you wouldn't get caught.

152

If you could gain the ability either to talk to animals or to see the future, which would you want?

If you could have anyone you know as a best friend, who would you pick?

If everyone in your class began teasing and picking on your best friend, and you knew that if you stayed friends everyone would start picking on you too, what would you do?

155

How would it make
you feel if most people
thought you were two years
younger than you are?
Two years **older**?

156

What do you think your **parents** should do for you without expecting to be **thanked**—for example, cooking your meals, buying your clothes, or taking you places? Do you think they would **agree** with you about this?

157

Have you had any personal experiences that make you believe in God? If so, have you ever doubted that they were real? If not, why do you think you haven't had them?

158

What is the best trick you ever played on someone?

159

Would you rather
learn to be a lot better
at **avoiding** bad,
upsetting things that might
happen, or a lot better at
handling your emotions
and feelings when such
things do happen?

If your parents didn't
care whether you got good
grades or not, would it
upset you? What do you know
more about than the kid who
gets the **best** grades
in your class?

161

What advice would you give a good friend who got very jealous of someone and started trying to act just like that person?

162

At what age should kids be able to wear whatever they want to school? At what age should they be allowed to go on dates unchaperoned?

163

What **grade** would you give your **teacher** for the overall job she does? For her patience? For her friendliness? For her handwriting?

How do you **feel** when you see someone who is disfigured or disabled? Could you be best friends with someone extremely **ugly**?

165

Why do you think
the most popular kids in
school are so popular?
In what ways do you think
you are better
than they are?

166

Is there anything so bad that if you found out your mother or father had done it, you'd call the police?

167

Do you try to act like your friends more than they try to act like you? Why?

Do you usually say what you **really** think or what you think other people want to hear? Do you think your life would be **better** or **worse** if you acted the other way more often?

Pretend you can
own only one pair of shoes
and have to choose between a
pair that looks **funny** but
feels great and one that looks
terrific but feels lousy.
Which would you **pick?**

170

If a rich kid wanted to buy your parents, how much would you ask for them—assuming you were willing to sell? Would you trade parents with any of your friends?

171

What's the best birthday party you ever had? If you could have any kind of party you wanted for your next birthday, what would you choose?

If you were riding your
bicycle and accidentally
ran into someone else's bike
and **wrecked** it—but
no one saw you—what
would you do?

173

Have you ever been humiliated by a teacher? If so, what happened?

174

Would you rather be a bed wetter, but have only your parents know about it, or never wet your bed but, because of a story someone made up about you, have everyone think you did?

175

Would it be worse

to spend a night all alone
in an **empty house** in
the woods, or to spend it
with a friend outdoors in a
thunderstorm?

176

If you had a chance to give a ten-minute speech to your whole school about anything you wanted, would you want to do it? What would you talk about?

177

What were you afraid of a few years ago that no longer bothers you?

178

If you were
given $1,000
to use to help other
people, how would
you spend it?

179

Would you rather have more **brothers and sisters** than you have now or fewer? What do you think is the **best** size for a family? Why?

180

When you grow up, do you think your parents will think you did better than they'd hoped you would or not as well?

181

If two kids in your class were caught bringing a gun or a knife into school and you had to determine their punishment, what would you choose? Would it matter if one of them was a friend?

182

Would you rather
your family **loved**
one another and always
showed how they felt—
sometimes fighting and
yelling, sometimes hugging
and kissing—or would you
prefer they loved one another
but **hid** their feelings
when they got upset?

183

If you could have your room clean and neat all the time or jumbled and messy, which would you choose?

184

What things scare you even though you know there is no reason to be afraid?

Have you ever—without
telling anyone—let someone
beat you at a game you
could easily have **won?**
If so, why?

Can you remember
a time you **succeeded**
when you thought you never
would? If so, how did it
feel? Would you rather try
ambitious things,
knowing you might fail,
or **easier** things you'll
almost certainly succeed at?

If you had to pick an **age** to be for your whole life, knowing you'd never grow **older,** what age would you pick?

188

If you were a **teacher** and the kids in your class wouldn't **listen** to you, what would you do? What if they **still** wouldn't listen?

189

Of all the things you could imagine
doing when you grow up, what would
most please your parents? What would
most disappoint them?

190

If you could live someone else's life for a
week—just to see what it was like—
would you want to? If so, who would it
be and why?

191

If a good friend came to your house with a black eye and—after you promised to keep it **secret**—told you his father had hit him, would you **tell** anyone? What if you didn't, and two months later the same thing happened **again?**

192

When was the last
time you felt completely
happy? What made
you feel so **good?**

If your babysitter said
she'd let you **stay up**
way past your bedtime if
you promised not to tell
anyone, would you
agree? If you did, what would
you **say** the next morning
when your mother asked
if you went to bed on time?

194

What's the worst accident you ever caused? Were you angrier at yourself than other people were, or was it the other way around?

195

What's your favorite daydream?

196

Have you ever been **blamed** for something you didn't do, yet not **told** on the person who really did it? If so, why didn't you tell?

If you could email any **famous** person and be sure they'd **read** and **answer** your note, who would you write to and what would you say?

198

What are the stupidest rules your parents have about what you must and must not do? What's so stupid about these rules?

199

If for one day you could do anything you wanted and not get punished no matter what it was, what would you do?

200

If you had to pick a **new** first name for yourself, what would you **choose?**

If eating nothing but
a **tasteless** food paste
for a year would make
you much **stronger** and
more **attractive,**
would you do it?

202

If a friend gave you a gift you didn't like, would you pretend you liked it?

203

Who is meanest to the kids in your neighborhood? If you knew you could get away with it, what trick would you play on him or her this Halloween? If you had to make up a story about how that person got to be so mean, what would it be?

204

What was your biggest failure?

205

If a friend threw a party and didn't invite you, what would you do?

If your parents decided
to let you watch any films
you wished, what kinds of
movies would you want to
see that are now off-limits?
What kinds would you
want to avoid until
you get older?

207

If you could go to a **special** hi-tech summer program that was really **hard** but helped you do a lot better in school, would you want to go? Would you rather just take a **pill** that made you smarter?

What do you think
your **family** would
miss the most about **you**
if you were to go live with
someone else?
What would you miss
most about them?

209

Do you believe in God? If not, why do you think so many people do? If so, what do you think God does all day?

210

If you could set your own allowance, how much would it be? Why did you pick that amount?

211

Have you ever seen
your mom or dad cry?
If not, how do you
think it would feel
to see that?

If you could gaze into
a **magic mirror**
and see exactly what's
happening anywhere in the
world, where would you
look and what do you
think you'd see?

213

If your teacher and your mother spent an afternoon discussing you, would you like to secretly listen in on their conversation? What do you think they would say?

214

Have you ever wished that something awful would happen to someone? If so, what was it, and what had they done to deserve it?

215

Would you rather
have to **repeat**
a grade in school
or gain a lot of
weight?

216

If you were given a
truth pill and asked
to describe each person
in your family, what
would you say?

217

What's the **best** thing
that could happen to you?
The **worst** thing?

218

What do you most dislike about
yourself? Do you think other people care
about it as much as you do?

219

When you and your friends play
together, do you prefer being at your
house or theirs? Why?

220

If you were going to be
stranded for ten years
on a tiny island paradise the
size of a football field, **who**
would you want with you?
Make believe you'd be in no
danger and would have
clothing, food, and shelter,
but **nothing** else.

What things do you see people doing just to **pass** the time and keep **busy?** What do you do just to pass the time?

222

If you could be the star of a reality TV show that followed your family 24-7 for a year, would you want to? Imagine that you would be a big celebrity, but that everyone would know everything about you and your family.

223

Who is your best friend? What is the worst thing about him or her?

224

Would you rather change
out of a **wet bathing
suit** in a crowded locker
room, or wait to change
at home an hour later?

225

If you could stop going to
school, would you?
What's the **worst**
thing about school?
What's the **best?**

226

Do you think it's fun to be a parent? If so, what do you think is the best thing about it? If not, why do you think people have kids?

227

If another kid does something wrong, are you more inclined to tell an adult, ignore it, or try to solve the problem on your own? For example, if you saw someone stealing things, would you tell a teacher? What would you do if a big kid spit on your lunch?

228

What's the
bravest thing
you **ever** did?

229

What is the **kindest**
thing you've ever done
for someone? Did anything
good come out of
your action?

230

If you bought something in a store and got a dollar too much in change, would you say anything?

231

If something happened to your parents and you had to go live with someone else for two years, who would you want to stay with?

232

What, if anything, about
your **family** would
you be **afraid** to
have your friends
find out?

233

Is there any question you would be afraid to ask someone because of the answer you might get?

234

If a teacher wanted to find out what you really thought and felt, how could he or she best get you to open up?

235

Do adults ever try
to get you to watch TV
or go online so you won't
bother them? If so,
how does that make you
feel? Would you do the
same thing if you were
babysitting or had
kids of your own?

236

If a friend's mother
died in an **accident,**
what would you say or do
to try to **comfort**
your friend?

237

How do you think your life would be **different** if you were three inches **taller?** Three inches **shorter?**

238

Has anyone done something so bad to you that you'd still like to get back at them if you could? What would you want to do to them?

239

Would it embarrass you to cry in front of your friends? Your father? Your little sister? If so, which would be worse and why?

240

If next year you could
go to any school
you wanted, would you
want to go somewhere
different? If so, how
do you think it would be
better there?

241

If friends of your parents served food that tasted disgusting and asked you how you liked it, what would you say? What do you think your parents would want you to say?

242

How do you think your life would change if someone in your family got really sick and had to stay in the hospital for a year?

243

If you had lots of **money**
and could use it **any**
way you wanted, what
would you do with it?

244

What do your
parents
do that most
embarrasses
you?

245

Pretend that three people in a hospital are dying: a one-year-old baby, a grandmother with lots of grandchildren who love her, and a teenager who works hard but just flunked out of high school. If you could save only one of them, who would you choose?

246

What foreign country have you heard the most about? What do you think it would be like to grow up there?

247

Would you like to have a brother who was just about the best brother you could imagine—friendly, smart, good at everything he tried, and close to you—if it meant that everyone would always talk about how great he was and not pay much attention to you?

248

What is one of your best tricks for getting attention from your parents? From your friends?

249

What really
gets on your
nerves?

250

Would you rather
be slender and athletic
but kind of dumb,
or fat and clumsy but
really smart?

251

Would you rather receive a gift you really wanted, or give your mother a gift she'd absolutely treasure?

252

There are lots of scary things in the world these days. What most worries you? What would you do if your fears came true?

253

Would you rather
have **no rules** at all
or live with the rules you
have? If there weren't **any**
rules, what would you
do differently?

254

If you were to give
your **mom** and **dad**
one tip on how to be
better parents, what
would you tell them?

255

If you knew that by never again eating
junk foods or candy, you'd live to be
eighty-five years old rather than
seventy-five, would you want to give up
those treats?

256

If you had a tiny camera the size of a
penny that could fly by remote control
and be your spy, who and what—if
anything—would you spy on?

257

If you could decide right now whether or not you will smoke cigarettes when you **grow up,** what would you decide? What about using drugs or drinking a lot? How do you think it would change your life if you did the **opposite?**

258

What is the scariest thing you've seen in a film or video game? Do you wish your parents had kept you from seeing it? Or would you like to see something even scarier?

259

What, if anything, do you think should be done to a kid caught illegally downloading lots of music and videos from the Internet? Would your answer be different if he or she were selling copies to friends?

260

What is the most
unfair thing about
the way your
family
is run?

261

When was the last time you **laughed** so hard you cried? If you could watch a movie that was so **funny** it made you laugh that hard for two whole **hours**, would you want to?

262

If your parents wanted everyone in the family to wear little monitor watches that would let any of you listen in on each other anytime you wanted, would you be willing to try this out for a year? How do you think it might change your family? Would you rather do this with your best friend instead?

263

If you had the power to choose someone and always be able to read his or her mind, who would you pick?

264

What is the most
important lesson about
life you've learned in the
past few years? How did
you learn it?

265

What's the funniest story you ever made up about why you weren't able to get your homework finished on time? Did anyone actually believe you?

266

If drinking a magic potion would make you never again feel sad no matter what happened, would you drink it?

267

Pretend that right
now you have to pick the
job you will have as
an adult. What's the
best job you can think of?
What's the worst?

If for an hour you
could ask your parents any
questions you wanted
and knew they'd tell you the
unvarnished **truth,** what
would you ask? Pretend
they'd **answer** every
question and then forget
they'd even talked to you.

ACKNOWLEDGMENTS

For their ideas, suggestions, and encouragement, I particularly thank Lillian McKinstry and Donald Ponturo. For her love and support, I thank Lori Fish. And I thank Douglas Balfour, Joseph Cambray, Kenny Cleveland, Sheila Garrigue, Jason Ide, Nettie Ide, Katy Fassett, Jane Stock, Jason Sullivan, Daniel Summer, Claudia Summer, Fred Weber, and the Denver Children's Museum.

For editorial assistance as well as ideas and suggestions, I thank Michael Cader and David Allender.

ABOUT THE AUTHOR

Questions have always been Dr. Gregory Stock's passion. He started asking them as a child and never stopped. His question books are mini-classics that have sold more than 4 million copies and been translated into 18 languages. He has a Ph.D. from Johns Hopkins and an MBA from Harvard, and has written more than 60 papers and three influential books on technology, ethics, and public policy in the life sciences. Stock has frequently spoken at schools and conferences, and he has made more than a thousand media appearances to discuss questions and values on shows ranging from *Oprah* and *Larry King* to *Science Friday, Nova,* and *Talk of the Nation*. He often appears on TV and radio as an authority on the implications of emerging life science and medical technologies, and he is now working to develop next-generation healthcare that is preventive, personalized, and patient-centered. His website is gregorystock.net. He has one child.